Dan Bob

THE MIND Of A RICH MAN

And What We Can Learn From Them!

By
Dan Bob

Copyright © Dan Bob, 2018

This original work of the author, the book and its texts, in whole or in part, shall not be reproduced, rephrased, paraphrased or taken extracts from; in print, electronic and any other form and shall not also be lent, shared, resold or circulated without the prior permission and written consent of the author. Please purchase a new copy for each person you intend to share the book with. Thank you for respecting the work of the author.

Legal Disclaimer

The contents of this book must not be considered as legal, financial or professional advice and must only be regarded as an information guide. You should seek the assistance of competent legal, accounting, investing, finance and other professionals and experts, if you require any of those services. So, this book is neither a replacement nor an alternative to professional services rendered by qualified professionals. Hence, we disclaim all liability incurred due to the use of the contents and the information contained in this book.

The Mind Of A Rich Man

While we have also put in our best of efforts to keep the information in the book as accurate and as close to reality as possible, we make no representations or warranties about the accuracy, completeness, correctness and applicability of the content and information in the book. Please consider yourself to have read and understood these terms before you purchase this book. By practicing and applying the information shared in this book, you are taking responsibility for your actions and you are doing so at your own risk.

CONTENTS

INTRODUCTION   06

CHAPTER I
Mind over Money   10

CHAPTER II
Using Other People's Money   20

CHAPTER III
Twisting the Terms to Riches   28

CHAPTER IV
High Paying Skills to Riches   32

CHAPTER V
How the Stock Market
Can Make You Rich   35

CHAPTER VI
Real Estate with No Money   38

CHAPTER VII
The Art of Talking Deals   45

CHAPTER VIII
Earn As You Sleep
(Passive Income Ideas)   54

CHAPTER IX
Earning Money "Like a Boss!" 59

CHAPTER X
Buying Out Businesses 62

CHAPTER XI
Seeing Money Differently 65

INTRODUCTION

Middle class people are conditioned to believe in the most primitive forms of employment, as most of the human species evolved from hunting and later from farming traditions. Both hunting and farming are straightforward economic activities. The linear relationship between "work and reward" or "input and output" can be firmly and easily established in these primitive or ancient economic activities.

On the other hand, the rich people are able to see the non-linear relationship created through value addition and they exploit the value, which, at times, is subjective. On the contrary, the middle class are conditioned to believe only in the objective world or the world of appearances.

The rich see through the subjective, work on it and exploit it. For example, there is no need for any economic or business sense in rendering your labor to produce a commodity or to offer a service. In hunting, there is no need for any economic or business sense. You just aim and hit. That's all you do.

However, economics begins when you begin to store value. A modern store of value is money.

When you begin to store food for later consumption, you add value because you add time, thought and effort. An economy catering to a growing population and evolving needs cannot depend on hunting or gathering food for each and every meal to survive.

Farming involves very limited economic sense, though it still does and that's where the need for an economic sense became activated than with hunting. In the earlier days, farmers probably aimed at achieving self-sufficiency through farming. With better tools and improved technology (which are activities that add value), surplus production could have been achieved. And surplus production, in turn, led to storage, distribution and trading. So, economics is basically a study of production, distribution and consumption, which comes from the need to store value.

So, the rich man does not engage in direct rendering of labor unless and until the task is of high value that will fetch him more value or money. The rich man sees beyond the visible, physical aspects of money and has an entirely different view of money. He knows other ways that can make him a lot of money and has plenty of calculations going on in his head on how to bring himself more money.

He trades value for money than labor. He is ahead of others in evolution. Many people debate whether rich people are truly smart and intelligent or if they are plain dumb. Such a debate is actually irrelevant, as rich people are more evolved in their understanding of the non-linear aspects on how money works and how their brain should work to get more value.

Getting rich involves shedding middle class values; to get ahead, to get more value and to make more money. It involves playing your cards close to your chest, posing a front, hiding your true feelings, sometimes revealing them at the right moment; not showing anger during provocative situations; getting into the grey areas and getting murkier; reading between the lines of a deal and making use of possibilities within them; finding loopholes and exploiting them and many more.

This book is designed to target the right areas in our brains to change the way we see the world, other people, money, business and finances. In order to target the right areas that cause changes, the book explains these concepts in a highly succinct manner.

So, let's take a quick tour to change the way we see and think about money to move us in the right direction that will eventually help us live financially better lives.

CHAPTER 1

Mind over Money

Money is governed by the mind. Most of what we earn in our lifetime and most of what we keep are both governed by the mind. So, we need to shed the social conditioning ingrained in us heavily by the society.

These limiting beliefs and social conditioning are typical of the middle class while a rich man's mind would be able to look around to see what's on the other side of what we (are normally forced to) see.

So, below are a few of the changes we need to make in ourselves and our minds to get rich:

1) Don't be too honest and righteous

A rich man knows when to be honest and when not to be. Complete honesty is counterproductive. Learning how to be dishonest a little is as important as being honest and hardworking.

2) Learn legal ways of tax avoidance

Note: We do not advocate nor support illegal tax evasion, as it is quite dangerous and, of course, illegal.

3) Use Other People's Money (OPM)

Don't feel shy or guilty about it. Using Other People's Money is the fastest way to get rich.

Don't be too honest and righteous

It pays rich karmic dividends, if you remain honest and righteous all your life. But even being only honest can cost you or someone else. Sometimes, it may even prove fatal to you or someone else, if you are way too honest.

Honesty is associated with huge monetary and financial loss. Behind every financially successful story, there is a lot of honesty and some bit of dishonesty. The some bit of dishonesty is like sugar. It just makes it taste better.

On the other hand, if you add too much sugar, you can't taste it.

Warren Buffett said, "Honesty is a very expensive gift. Don't expect it from cheap people!" This is so very true, as we have evolved from crude, direct theft to subtle ways of getting people to part with their money.

In fact, it turned so subtle that it now is almost honest. The strategies businesses use to get you to part with your money may or may not always be honest. However, it is legal, honest, just and fair! You, as a consumer, reserve the right to say no and no one can force you than try to trick you into consuming something by employing sales tactics. This is far better than direct theft. This is economy, business and this is how companies and countries survive and thrive.

In order to better understand what Buffett says, let's take Buffett himself as an example. I think Buffett said this to mean the CEOs who have to be honest, if he should want to invest in a company.

Honesty should be the very first ingredient on the checklist, should Buffett invest in a company. The CEO must be able to make proper use of the resources that are mostly public money or other investors' money and not misuse or misappropriate any of them.

At the same time, he must be efficient at getting a fair deal in everything including the purchase of raw materials or switching to someone who takes a lesser pay for the same quality product or service. He may also need to know how to legally minimize taxes and benefit himself and his stakeholders, even though he would also be using a Chief Financial Officer.

However, you can see average people are made to excessively believe in honesty and straightforwardness. Being too straightforward in business can prove to be costly, in fact very counterproductive. The ideas of honesty and straightforwardness come out of socialistic loyalty. It's a sort of conditioning. This does not, though, mean that you must be dishonest enough to flout the laws.

A straightforward attitude limits your possibilities and blinds you to many other opportunities that aren't harmful to anyone but that which you can gain from.

You may sometimes have to think beyond rigid protocols, rules, etc. and even break some of them. You can give someone what he wants, though not the best of its variety. You must reserve what you want, the best for yourself, and what you will likely benefit the most from.

You should also be able to short change someone i.e. pay him lower than what he expects—to get some work done. Though not to the extent of making it difficult for him to lead a normal life, you must still be able to pay a lower price and get the same amount of work done.

A picture is worth a thousand words but a movie scene is worth a million or even a billion words. What I've said in so many words could be understood through just four lines of a movie dialogue. That's why movies are a very powerful medium. No one could have put it better than in the dialogue below, from the movie "The Aviator":

Though a popular film, for those who aren't familiar, Leonardo DiCaprio plays Howard Hughes who, in the scene, hires Noah Dietrich, played by John C. Reilly, his second-in-command Chief Executive Officer.
Though the movie is based on the real life story of the eccentric business magnate Howard Hughes, the scene and dialogues could be fictional. That's probably why it's quite brilliant:

Howard: Good. Now you made what, uh, five thousand two hundred dollars a year your last job; I'll pay you ten thousand!

Noah: Guess I'll be working twice as hard!
Howard: You'll be workin' four times as hard; I just got you half price, Mr. Dietrich. Welcome aboard! (Logan)

This kind of shrewdness and smartness in matters of money and most things in life can sure make you rich. You should appeal to people's base emotions as greed, jealousy and desire to get what you want to get rich quick.

Using Pretexts

Similarly, if you want to get a job done, sometimes, you may have to substitute a false reason, when you assign the job to someone.

Even if you want someone to do something for you, it is better to use a pretext over why you want it done for you.

If he finds that the work is going to fetch too much money for you, he will likely try to charge you more. If you say you are going to get nothing out of it, he will scale down his remuneration. By employing such strategies and tactics, you can make yourself comfortable with more cash that you can keep, save, invest and let it grow.

Tax Avoidance to Grow Wealth

The real trick in avoiding taxes is in not attracting most of the usual taxes on your income by changing the terms through which you get paid.

One such trick is to receive payments via a (personal) corporation, a business instead of receiving them as an individual. By receiving payments as a business, you can spend money from the business account for fuel, (business) lunch, etc.

Usually, when it comes to corporations, Revenue Service tax officials follow strict rules, laws and protocols to avoid tax fraud, as a CEO handles other people's (investors') money.

A personal corporation, on the other hand, can give you some pre-tax dollars to carry out some daily and long term expenses before filing taxes. Since you, your spouse and or your family are going to be the only stakeholders, a personal corporation like an S Corp can give you a lot of tax benefits.

An S Corp, especially, avoids double taxation, as the shareholder files returns as an individual and pays taxes on profits and dividends personally received by him.

Robert Kiyosaki, author of the book "Rich Dad Poor Dad", who has also been a mentor of finance for a whole generation since the 90s, has often hinted at the possibility of passing off personal expenses as business expenses. For example, your business can pay for anything from your fuel to a car used for business purposes. Beware also of the possibility that Revenue Service tax offices in your country might keep a strict vigil and your expenses should look like they are legitimate business expenses. And even though the car was purchased for your business, you can employ the same for personal use. Robert Kiyosaki was quite brilliant in highlighting this loophole.

Some people were confused and took this advice too literally. You can't pass off every personal expense as a business expense.
However, you can put more pre-tax dollars to use for personal expenses by running a personal corporation (Kiyosaki 79-90). Additionally, you can also avoid personal income tax by receiving payments on your company name than on yourself.

Compare the same with an employee of any organization who has to buy everything from gas to car and even candies with post-tax income. It really is a sad thing that way. And saving up on 30-40% of your taxes is a huge investment in itself.

Robert Kiyosaki's argument is that governments allow businesses such loopholes as they want them to grow in size and provide more employment, which solves the problem of unemployment in any country.

An economy grows only if the people living in the country are productive in one way or another.

So, as businesses help increase productivity and GDP (Gross Domestic Product) and help the economy grow by providing employment, Kiyosaki argues that businesses will always be allowed such loopholes. And even if the governments don't, according to Kiyosaki, rich people will always find a way of their own to reduce and avoid taxes. And to make things better, most countries of the world consider a business as another person. So, even if you own equity in many incorporated businesses, you can own a personal corporation that owns those businesses for you instead of owning them as an individual.

This can also be a nice way of avoiding personal liability and litigation to avoid losing your personal wealth.

Almost all Governments reinforce a sort of socialistic mindset. They are usually against individuals gaining and hoarding wealth. But most governments do allow large corporations to operate. They are their economic reformist arms that carry out economic activity, develop the infrastructure, provide employment, etc.

Growth of large corporations reflects as good governance. So, governments encourage corporates to hoard money and not individuals. The government still keeps an eye on that money but corporate firms do their best to protect it, as does Apple, stashing away hundreds of billions of dollars outside of the United States.

So, the bottom line is that you should change your attitude towards money on what it truly is, how money is made and how you spend, save or invest therefrom!

Leveraging or Using Other People's Money is discussed in the next chapter.

CHAPTER 2

1) OPM – Other People's Money – Leverage

"Money is always Other People's. It's never Yours!"

Who pays you? Other people! Who does it come from? Other people! Who buys your goods? Other people! Who gives you loans? Other people! Who invests in your business? Other people!

Financial leverage is one of the best ways to get rich. We do not always have enough money to invest in any asset, when we begin investing. We may not have enough money to buy just one Berkshire Hathaway Class "A" share but we can do so with leverage, if the rate of interest is lower than the projected growth of the stock price. (Not to be taken literally, you may find better options for a stock, as large companies post lower rates of growth).

Warren Buffett has also famously spoken against leveraging (borrowing) to buy stocks, as it is a bad idea to buy stocks with borrowed money. But leveraging other people's money by way of capital is probably the "only" way you have to do it. That's the best practice.

You may even be able to get money from someone else, which a lot of people may think is difficult. However, it only matters on what terms you get the money from them. That's why you should twist the terms and pose a different reason or purpose. There are legal provisions for you to get money and leverage other people's money.

As an individual, you can leverage and use other people's money by way of promises. I've been able to learn the art of appealing to base emotions as greed and fear by sounding reasonable. Typically, I have been logical in the way I think and talk. Naturally, I had my left brain work really well. Later, sensing that my right brain capacities were very limited, I started working on getting my right brain up to speed.

So, I was able to talk logically and still work out the abstract to relate to people's emotions to get them to pay in my terms.

Leveraging can be good as well as bad depending on what terms you took the money from the other person.

Earning money simply means to receive money without any liability attached to it or to have full ownership of the money. You can play with the terms as partial ownership (if such a thing were to exist) or entrusting you with the money to benefit both of you.

When it comes to entrusting money, there are several ways you can get someone to trust you and pay you:

1) You can simply make a promise of returns and get someone to hand you some cash.

2) You can receive money as inheritance

3) You can incorporate a company and issue them shares for the money they invest

4) You can do the required groundwork for someone to help him buy properties or assets and handle his money. (A person with an ordinary middle class mindset would do it as a job, while a business minded person would ask for a stake (5-30-50%) in the properties he buys for him.

If the amount is huge, you can also do the same for commissions running up to 5%. Usually, asking for stake or commissions convinces the payer that you are genuine. If you say you do not want any stake or commissions, he might assume that you are going to defraud him of the whole amount.)

5) Seek help

1, 3, 4 and 5 have all worked for me. It depends on what kind of people you are talking to and their temperament. When none of promises, issue of shares, investment management worked for me with a client, finally I sought his help and it did work out.

Leveraging capital as investment using other people's money does come with some obligation—the fulfillment of some purpose. There is no full-on debt liability as in a loan. So, while seeking money or funds, you should be able to play with different terms and get it in a way that reduces your liability but speeds up your growth.

That's probably the best use of the term "leverage" and banks have probably used the term to trick people into piling on debt.

Still due to the promise you make to another person, when leveraging, you have to ensure that you can comfortably leverage and earn profits from that particular property or asset.

Leveraging is mostly useful in real estate. Day Traders and (Short Term) Swing Traders use leverage (margin) for the stock market. Average people use leverage to buy cars and gadgets, which mostly helps them run into bad debt to ruin their finances.

At the same time, I would suggest that one not be afraid to take on debt for business or any other purpose. Sometimes, debt may be vital. If you know you are capable of easy repayment and if you take the right amount as a loan, you can double your money and build your wealth.

Even if you want to buy a car, I would also suggest leverage as an option. If you want to buy a $25000 car and if you have only $15000, I would advise you to buy the $25000 car than a $12000-15000 car. This is only if you have the necessary cash flow to pay off the loans each month. You can also find a lower interest car loan or switch to one later. It is always better to not spend all your money at once. You may even buy a $11000 car but you may still do so out of a loan than to pay all the cash up front.

You can invest the rest to keep the money with you as well as to let it grow.

Some people factor in the interest rates and having to pay higher than you would, if you took a loan. But a loan is for those who have the cake already and want to eat it too. This means that only when you are sure of your income or cash flow, it is advisable to take a loan. You can leverage for the real estate, if you know you can resell it quickly, if its value will appreciate and if you are sure about getting rent from the property.

However, leveraging to buy personal stuff will always add to your burden and you will be less in control of the cash you own. Still, I think leveraging to buy something is highly beneficial than to pay all the cash you have upfront. C0nservative people are conditioned to believe that they should "live below their means" and hence opt for the $12000-15000 car by default. They might also be willing to pay all the money upfront merely in order to avoid taking on debt. Of course, the problem is just the opposite. People take on too much debt and go broke. You can leverage wisely to gain momentum in your life, especially if you want to speed up your growth. Still, it is good to be prudent, when it comes to leveraging.

You should be able to afford more than what you have by way of leveraging, if and only if you know how to make financial sense in the future.

Who is Leveraging For?

Leveraging is for everyone. Whoever takes on debt to buy personal stuff can leverage the same for business. Leveraging is for those who do not have any money as well as those who already have (a lot of) money or wealth. With leveraging, you either create new money, as economies do, or double your money like magic.

You can leverage when you have a business plan, a real estate deal or any activity that can bring you income or cash flow or for other relatively smaller and or insignificant expenses. With the vision and promise of an income, it can get easy for you to leverage either through loans or investments. If you already have enough money or wealth, you can double your money or wealth by way of leveraging.

Leveraging can increase the speed at which you execute your business plans.

Trying to find your own money or using your own money can become frustrating and time consuming. It may slow down the process. Leveraging is the best way to speed up your business and make profit.

I come across a lot of people who say that they have a business plan but can't start up a business because they don't have enough money to invest. This is a very faulty idea. In addition to leveraging the required capital, you can also leverage land (space), labor and equipment as well.

Get space or equipment for free, get donated, take a computer from a friend who doesn't use it anymore and utilize someone's skills or knowledge in return for sweat equity. Do a quid pro quo and get work done in return for some other work you can do for them. All such activities can be called leverage. Almost all businesses and economies grow with one form of leverage or the other.

Leveraging is discussed in detail further in a later chapter.

CHAPTER 3

Twisting the Terms to Riches

This is another most important fundamental attitude shift you need to make to earn money. Assuming you sign up for a project, you should be able to change the terms and get paid for and under a different reason than receiving a straightforward remuneration.

Payment Terms/Payment Schedule

I used to get 100% project cost or price well in advance for my business projects. Most of my clients pay 50%, 33% or at least 25% upfront. You may think a 100% upfront payment is not possible. Well, it is, if you play clever tricks as giving your client an offer using a pretext. I knew one of my clients was quite wealthy but had the attitude of seeking more bang for his buck. So, I told him, "I will deliver twice the amount of work for what you will pay, if you pay today!" using an occasion as Christmas or Independence Day for an offer!

He was only too willing to pay, as he could get twice the work done for the same amount he was going to pay me anyway. To me, the discount was just the price I had been doing the work for, just some one to two years ago.

Sometimes, choosing whether to get paid twice, thrice or four times on a project can ensure you make profit midway through the project. You can avoid loss and you won't have to wait till the project is complete to profit from it. The client will also find it comfortable to split the payment into three or four schedules than one or two.

He will assume by default that you are making it comfortable for him whereas you will be making it comfortable for yourself. Of course, all these work on an each-client, per-project basis but you can take a pattern and work out something each time to fit each client.

If I get paid 25 or 33% in each schedule, I profit before the completion of the project. Split your project into processes and schedules or structure your payments either before or after completion of each process. With a 25 0r 33% schedule, I make a profit within the third payment and the fourth brings me the whole margin.

By splitting the payment, you can also make it seem like a lot less in the payer's eyes. That's another great trick, which one can use at the right time and at the right place. Loans and profiting from loans happen in much the same way. You can easily create the illusion of paying less in someone's mind by breaking the payment down into smaller pieces.

If you pay $1800 each and every month for 30 years for your home valued at $300,000, at the time of purchase, y0u will be paying more than $650000. Some people only look at how low they can pay each month but they can't see how much they are paying in the long run. Businesses usually exploit this illusion. If a borrower pays a lender $1000-2000 each and every month for over 30 years, the lender gets a life while the borrower loses it. He enjoys 30 years of passive income because the loaned money is an asset for the lender and liability for the borrower. So, splitting or breaking your payment into multiple schedules can be a very rewarding technique.

Perhaps, the best lessons or skills one can learn in the process of getting rich is how to sell, how to talk a deal, how to make the deal profitable for you, etc.

Good business people play within the terms, find loopholes and make deals profitable for them. Eventually, though, it's also important to create a win-win situation at any cost.

Also, getting sales to happen is important as well. Find what a client is lacking in your area of expertise, which the client himself is not knowledgeable about. At times, it doesn't matter, if your knowledge exceeds your client's. Find something lacking in anything ranging from a machine to a website. Offer to upgrade it. Bag the project.

When it comes to cell phone plans, you can see how mobile carriers get you to pay more. Once when I asked for a lower plan, the sales personnel explained me that I would get very low data, low text and low talk for the lower plan. So, I told her to not change it and let me remain on the same higher plan. You can sell not only by providing your customers what they want but also by taking it away from them.

Chapter 4

High Paying Skills to Riches

What you can do for someone else translates into money. A builder friend of mine said he could walk away with a cool $25000-50000 by building a house. A software developer could get paid in hundreds of thousands of dollars, if he made a piece of software or application for another firm. He can also find an investor and make a software or application product of his own and sell the application to make tons of money.

Leveraging high paying skills requires that you acquire a certain skill, talent or education that you can use to become rich. The skill, ability or talent can come either through a professional degree or certification or even without any academic education. Sometimes, you can undertake large processes and huge responsibilities, if you would like to make the big bucks.

All these can help you earn a lot of money but getting rich is a different thing altogether. So, getting rich can become easy, if you invest the big bucks you make.

Even those who do not work for someone else as employees but execute projects for others do not realize that they do not become rich till they live off a second or multiple sources of income. Unless and until they invest and if they depend only on that single source of income, they will one day or the other fall short of meeting their daily needs and requirements. They will then begin to become desperate to find work and sadly they may not, at times.

However, those who develop high paying skills have a significant advantage compared to those who get paid only salaries. Those who take up large responsibilities also get paid higher. If the frequency of your projects increases, you will always remain richer, though that's not the best way to get rich. You will have enough of a cash flow, which can make you feel comfortable with matters of money.

Your limited physical and mental capacities — as is the case with all human beings — is compensated by the large fee, margin or profit you make from the deal or project. So, acquiring a high paying skill can and does promise some form of large sized income.

Since it is more than what you need to make a living, you can invest a large part of the money.

Ironically, those who earn the least amount of money have mostly saved or invested for years and become rich. Those who got paid the highest salaries most often went broke.

Most of the singers, athletes, etc. went broke within a couple of years they quit their careers. Some did even within a few months. Though getting paid higher salaries doesn't mean you get rich, it's a huge advantage, which you can use to build wealth quite easily than someone who gets paid low wages.

Getting rich has to do with building wealth by buying or owning cash flow generating assets. So, a large monthly income or fee enhances your possibilities, abilities and even leveraging possibilities to own large cash flow generating assets.

Chapter 5

How the Stock Market Can Make You Rich

Stocks are one of the best forms of paper assets. They may be difficult to pick but they are also the most rewarding.

Invest when the market value or market capitalization of a company is low but if you believe that the company will grow a 100 to a 1000 times its current size.

There are many other metrics to consider like PE Ratios, PEG, RoE, RoCE, Debt-to-Equity Ratios, Operating Profits, Net Profits, Dividends, Earning per Share (EPS), Price-to-Equity Ratios, Price-to-Book Ratios, etc.

Although we can explain in detail what these terms mean, which we may be willing to do on a separate book for the stock market, you can also read Benjamin Graham's "The Intelligent Investor: The Definitive Book on Value Investing" (Graham) and similar works to know more on the subject.

Stocks and mutual funds, however, are two different things. A mutual fund is for those who do not want to take on the hassle involved in picking stocks. However, you may have to pick a fund that performs the best among all the other funds.

There are a couple of ways to invest in the stock market. One is the fundamental investing approach and the other is a trading approach. In the former, you analyze the true value or net worth of a company by going through its balance sheets. You analyze both the company's book value (present value) as well as intrinsic value (future value).

The public opinion on the company on what price per share they are willing to pay to own the stock is the market price. The market price multiplied by the total number of outstanding shares is the total market capitalization of the company. Value investors buy a stock when the market price (public opinion) of the stock is lower than its actual value in the present (book value or net worth).

They buy and hold the stock till its market price goes disproportionately higher than its net worth per share (book value) or if the Price to Earnings (PE) Ratio gets too high.

Other reasons for selling include changes in management, poor performance, loss of brand value, competition, etc. But value investors are usually buy and hold investors who remain invested for the longest term possible.

Value investing may not be for everyone, if your fund size is smaller. Personally, I would suggest swing trading (short term trading) targeting a 10-15% rise in the price of a stock anywhere from 10-15 days to a month or a couple of months. A 10-15% profit in 10 to 15 days or a month to a couple of months is a huge profit compared to a measly bank interest of 2%.

Be careful that when you aim at such profit, do not buy on margin (leverage) and be forced to sell for a loss, when the stock price goes down, after you buy the stock. Buy on cash and hold till you get a profit. You can be sure that your returns will be much higher than bank interest.

Many people have made themselves a 1000 times richer by investing in the stock markets. The simple verdict is that the stock market is the best investment, if you learn how to pick, when to buy a particular stock, how long to hold and when to sell.

Chapter 6

The No Money Real Estate (Leverage in detail)

House Flipping with No Money

House flipping with no money is a Wild Wild West thing, as someone who has that bent of mind can pull it off quite easily. This does not mean that others shouldn't try it out. In fact the idea behind the book is for the reader to know the nuances of money, wealth and finance and to practice them. So, we would only encourage readers to try these tips out of their own will.

Leveraging for the real estate is neither easy nor difficult. We can neither be dismissive of the idea nor can it be an everyday event for everyone. However, the same might even happen at least once in your life, even without your knowledge. All of us have to live in houses and of course, we have seen at least one person in our lives who has wanted to sell his house property off immediately for some reason.

Real estate experts also advise finding distressed real estate assets and properties to flip.

I've found it easy to talk to my immediate business partners, co-directors, etc. into investing in a property. So, let's go through a few of the ways through which you can buy a real estate property with no money:

a) Buying properties as a real estate corporation

Buying a real estate property as a real estate corporation can help you own stake/equity in not just one property but many. When I pitched my holdings and investments business, I did not invest any of my own money but I was the one who put forth the project or business idea and had the modus operandi in picking stocks and running the business. So, I was entitled to get a lot of sweat equity, as I saw fit. I took 33.3% initially, whose value might appreciate through premium pricing, as we grow or bring in more investors and or invest in the business ourselves.

Similarly, you can propose to start a real estate firm where in you will hold a certain stake.

Let's say you go for another co-founder to incorporate your real estate business and you can secure a 50% stake for yourself.

Now, you can pore over many real estate property deals and buy them through your company. Then, you can flip it and take a share of the profits. In fact, there is a lot more you can do with a business than doing anything as an individual. A legal entity gives you more opportunities and reliability among other investors while pooling in funds.

Buying it for a company also creates a common interest than if the property were owned by a single person. It creates enough equitable interest from all the participants in their effort towards procuring and selling it. Nobody feels left out including you. Buying properties as a real estate company is one of the best ways to acquire real estate property without spending any money on your own.

b) Partnerships and Loans

Without incorporating a company, which is my idea and which I believe works better, you can also form partnerships with another person. You can talk a certain stake or profit share in the property and use your investor partner's money to buy and flip the property.

Alternatively, you can take hard loans for a high rate of interest and or private money with a low rate of interest from friends, family and or acquaintances to buy real estate assets to flip.

c) Buying a Property with Little Cash

Another easy way to buy real estate assets requires some cash on your part. You can make a down payment of about one tenth or one twentieth of the price of the property. How low you are able to pay depends mostly on your negotiation skills. You can then rehab the property and sell it for a good price, making a margin.

Buying a real estate property with a down payment as low as 3.5-5% its price is the best example of leveraging. You can then sell the property to another buyer and make a margin without ever getting close to paying its full price. This can be applied on many other fronts on many other assets. In fact, almost all of the assets could be procured this way and sold this way.

Stocks, for example, could be purchased with leverage of up to one fifth to one tenth their price.

However, there is also a certain interest paid with leveraging. It is also risky, if you don't exit at the right time and keep paying high rates of interest.

Some buy and sell a house even within a week. You find a seller and a buyer and get some money advanced through the buyer. You, then, pay the seller, add a margin and sell the buyer for a different price from anywhere within a week to a month.

Getting rich is in making things work. Leveraging is one of the best financial tools that you can use to quicken your process of getting rich. It works best in real estate, stock markets, entrepreneurship and businesses.

Leveraging happens through your ability to talk deals. You can make things work out of thin air with leveraging, just as governments and central banks print money out of thin air.

However, it should also be understood that we are not the government. So, we can't probably get away with leveraging as much as governments do. When governments borrow in excess from another country, it led to wars and invasions before the 1950s. Now, it may result in favorable trade agreements that benefit the lender country.

As individuals and at the levels of power that we command, we are more vulnerable and are easy to fall prey to our own greed and the financial system. We may put ourselves in such situations out of ignorance and powerlessness.

The system is sometimes an illusion. When there is an economic downturn, your asset size or the value of your assets will shrink and will fetch you only less cash to pay off your loans. So, even asset values are not fixed, concrete or solid, as we believe them to be. Even your net worth is still just a number assigned to you. That's how ridiculous the concept of wealth, money and assets are.

The economy of production and consumption are real because we live of them and enjoy them by way of consumption. However, the manufacturing of every product requires some service. This is not also to say that all services are illusion but valuing them mostly is. So, all leveraging, stock investments, real estate investments should be based on underlying economic activities. If there is going to be no economic activity with leveraging or if your cash flow or income is significantly lower than your debt, you are sure to lose wealth big time.

So, leveraging with prudence is a really great and faster way to get rich, especially when you are starting out. And leverage does not have to mean only debt and we have not meant it in this book to mean only debt.

Chapter 7

The Art of Talking Deals

Business can hardly happen without talking deals. Much of what I've done in business resulted out of talking deals with others. You have to talk deals with creditors, investors, banks, landlords, raw material suppliers, equipment suppliers, customers, buyers and clients. So, basically there is no business without talking deals.

"Trump: The Art of the Deal" (Trump and Schwartz) is a good place to start. Despite widespread criticisms on Donald Trump, the book is a bestseller with some great reviews. The Art of the Deal is a biography of sorts that details Trump's childhood, life, business, entrepreneurship and the deals he has made.

By reading the book, you may get an idea of how Donald J. Trump was able to create a successful brand out of his name and leverage the same on almost all types of businesses. Trump's leveraging ability is a clear sign that he was able to make money out of thin air.

If you are able to make even a dollar out of thin air, you should consider yourself rich because with the butterfly effect, it can only multiply, unless you act against it yourself. Passive income feels very exciting, even when you make only a $100 of passive income. You can only know what it feels like, only when you make even a small amount of passive income.

The book "Trump: The Art of the Deal" begins by detailing what Donald Trump does throughout the day at his office. It might appear that most of his business happens over the phone. He keeps talking deals for most parts of the book.

All over the world, Trump's name has served as a brand on almost all types of businesses and industries.

He leveraged his brand (name) or "name as a brand" into real estate (Trump Towers), hotels, neckties, suits, shoes, cuff links, shirts, deodorants, t-shirts, bed linens, teddy bears, key chains and even "Trump branded urine tests" (Anthony, Sanders and Fahrenthold). Besides objects, even living creatures as a moth and a sea urchin were also named after Trump (Nazari) (Thompson). Of course, we believe he doesn't get paid for those creatures.

The most amazing thing about all of it is that Donald Trump did not use even a penny of his own money. He leveraged other people's efforts, aspirations, work, products, services, marketing, etc. to pay himself. That's surely something to learn from!

Talking a deal is another way of twisting the norms, rules and finding loopholes. Smudge and distort the established norms to create an entirely different picture. My first deal came through the internet. I got someone from another country invest in my business by communicating only via emails.

In another deal, I had investors invest merely for my knowledge of the stock markets. I was able to make a good pitch of the general prospects of the stock market and what we could do to exploit it to the maximum. It worked.

Similarly, I hardly liked someone telling me that I needed some experience or track record to get others to pay me or to invest in my business. That, to me, was very old school. I also guess some of you might believe the same. So, I will tell you how contrarian ideas work and how twisting of logic (that people currently believe in) can work in your favor with three of my real life examples:

Example 1:

One of my cousins said, "How will you get someone to invest when there are thousands of others who are so very experienced and competing already?" Partially, I felt he was correct. At the same time, I also felt very sick to my stomach over how limiting and old school his thinking was.

I said, "Look! I already got two others interested in my company, even before we incorporated it. They're investing. And you don't seem to understand what we call "disruption." When fresh blood enters an industry, it is the older ones that have to fear losing their market share or monopoly. They also have to fear innovation and the entry of new dynamics in the way they've been doing business!"

Example 2:

A friend in the Middle East did not invest with me, despite repeated requests. He said he had already invested plenty of money in Dubai. Sometime later, I asked him what he invested in and what returns they were fetching. As he replied, I told him how he had less control over his investments.

I said they were neither personal nor customized. I also told him how I could get him better returns. He gave in.

Example 3:

We had an unused office space that was rented by another director of our holdings firm. He was using it for some other business of his own. Suddenly, the projects that came his way came to a halt. So, he told me to make use of the space and put it to some use.

I could have but the space itself was not going to benefit me in any way. So, I did not take up the offer. At the same time, I was already planning to run a digital marketing business. Since I have been looking after the holdings company, I would not be able to look after the Digital Marketing business though I was interested in it, as it promised steady revenue.

So, I called a friend of mine who I knew was into Digital Marketing a few years ago. I asked him to head the business and run it, while we would provide him with the space, computers, equipment, labor, etc. I was talking a bit low key because I did not want him to believe we were investing big, for him to expect the salary of a CEO or a Manager.

Instead, I said he could take sweat equity, as he already knew how to make money through the business. He agreed. So, we gave him 33% sweat equity in the digital marketing business, while the rest of the 66% would be held by our holdings company.

While talking about this a few days ago, one of our directors said we wouldn't be able to start a few of the processes because we would have to pay. I didn't believe in it. I didn't say anything back then. If I had thought in straight terms as salary, wages, etc., without the attitude towards leveraging anything, we wouldn't have been able to start the digital marketing business.

So, a shift in perspective and twisting of the existing terms and logic are very important. If I had thought that the one who managed the business had to be paid regular salaries, I wouldn't have been able to start the business for over six months. But with a slight change in how we see things and by changing the payment terms, I would now be able to leverage the space (which is rented by another director) and also get a manager to run the business (leveraging human labor). Not only money (capital), even land, labor, equipment and all that you need to run a business can be leveraged.

So, all you need is a new logic or an idea to override and disrupt the existing setup, belief or establishment. That's how most of the billionaires we see today succeeded in their businesses. Amazon, Apple (Mac), Microsoft, iPhones, Sony's Walkman, Sony Televisions, all of them won through disruption. Not only in businesses, even political changes happen by way of disruption. If you base your disruption on facts and truth that other people have missed taking note of, your thesis will look even more powerful and convincing.

Large establishments can keep growing for an indefinite period of time with all their power and might but they will also reach saturation sooner than a new entrant into the business. New entrants in an industry are always a threat to the existing players.

With innovation, you will be surprised how existing competition is uprooted to make way for you because nature loves innovation, innovators and new ways of doing things. Your ability and flexibility to adapt will sure break the rigid structure of an existing corporation.

The most important thing to learn out of this is that not everything is carved in stone in this world. It all is in your head.

If you merely change the way you see something and see it from a different angle, you will find plenty of new opportunities that the whole wide world has failed to see.

So, you make way for yourself, when you see something from a completely different vantage point. Even if the reality you believe in is based on fact, you can create new facts, as long as it is not hard science. You can create new logic and override existing ones. That's how the world works. The world uses such multiple dimensions to evolve. What Donald Trump did was to create a fresh perspective, a new way of approaching things, a change in attitude from the usual way we are used to seeing things. It wasn't probably something entirely new but he was able to leverage the concept and exploit it to the point of saturation.

Despite his Television appearances, he probably had little else to make a brand out of his name, when he proposed the idea. Initially, an executive laughed it off, as you can read from the article cited above.

Sometimes, all branding takes is reinforcement whether or not it truly carries any value in the first place.

Donald Trump may not be sued for lack of quality in a product for lending his name. And the rest of us are used to asking, "What's in a name?"

Chapter 8
Passive Income Ideas
"Earn as You Sleep!"

Passive income is one of the best ways to get some cash flow going but was hitherto unknown to most parts of the world. Except for a Warren Buffett who kept pinball machines in barber shops all over Washington D.C., not many would have realized its true power.

But the birth of the personal computers, the rise of the internet and the digital era has given rise to many passive income possibilities. As the manufacturing sector took the backseat and as jobs went on the decline, those who couldn't find jobs started finding passive income opportunities.

Some people made the best use of it through the internet. Online payment facilities and downloads of software products began to revolutionize the passive income universe.

eBay was perhaps the first to help the average internet user earn money by posting their (used) products online. Amazon came up with almost the first of the affiliate programs. Google, then, came up with AdSense, which changed the name of the game.

Even now Google AdSense is one of the best passive income ideas, if you know how to get it to work. YouTube further enhanced the possibility of earning through AdSense, as more and more people started watching videos on their smartphones.

Amazon Kindle, eBooks and Print-On-Demand books revolutionized how books were published, marketed and sold. Thanks to technology, now even a single copy of a book can be made to order. It avoided the loss publishing houses incurred due to mass printing. Those who could write but did not know how to find a publisher are now able to self-publish their books.

Self-Publishing a book is also very easy. Perhaps, earning royalties out of sale of eBooks is relatively easier than a few other methods. AdSense may take a long time for approval and may need plenty of content on a website or a certain amount of traffic or views before it can show ads on your website or videos.

Using YouTube to monetize your videos is a better option as well. You can also create entertainment and infotainment apps with certain features and functions and allow free usage. You can put ads on the app to monetize it.

Affiliate marketing too does work for some. If you do tech reviews of gadgets like mobile phones, laptops and pads, affiliate marketing can help you earn a fairly good amount of passive income. Some travel bloggers have lived their travel life out of the money earned from their travel blogs through affiliate marketing. They sell travel gear through affiliate links within text and video reviews, brand comparisons, etc.

Selling physical products too on Amazon can also be very rewarding in terms of cash flow. If you can procure products at wholesale prices or less, you can list them for sale on Amazon. You can sign up for Fulfillment by Amazon (FBA) (where you send products to their warehouse and they complete the sale) or Easy Ship (where they pick up the product from you for each order) or ship on your own through a third party courier or logistics service.

It feels like everything is on auto-pilot, when Amazon takes the order, picks up the product from you and credits you with the margin each and every week.

Currently, selling online courses of technical and non-technical soft skills via sites like Udemy have been in vogue. If you have expertise in any field, subject or profession, you can make a course material and put it up for sale on Udemy. Users will pay you and download your material.

Another popular way is to make a website that will be very useful and valuable for your audience and getting them to subscribe to pro-versions. You can do the same on apps. If people think that your app or website improves and adds value to their lives in some way, they are sure to register or subscribe to paid versions of your app.

Currently, enabled by technology, peer-to-peer lending on a safe platform with guaranteed returns is another attractive way to earn passive income. Though there is some risk in lending, you can sit back and watch your money grow each and every week or month. The platforms ensure that fair transactions take place, though it's not entirely free of risks.

The biggest advantage of peer-to-peer lending is that you can even lend a few hundreds to a few thousand dollars and make a profit out of it.

Chapter 9

The Entrepreneur's Route to Riches

Earn Money "Like a Boss!"

Till 2010, most people tried to be entrepreneurs. That was when Mark Zuckerberg and Jeff Bezos became prominent. Mark Zuckerberg is the best example of how to get rich the fastest way. However, a Facebook doesn't happen each and every day and some of his skills, hard work and dedication could be unparalleled and unmatched, despite a lot of other criticisms on him.

Many people get rich not because they are doing a lot of things in the world outside of them. They get rich because they leverage their brains. Your brain is the best leverage you can use. That's also why we have also emphasized the importance of "High Paying Skills" in this book. All the money that you are going to make is already made inside of you in your head, in your brain.

There is also the butterfly effect. Some hobby in your childhood or some pastime has the possibility of turning into a large business or enterprise. Even some habits have the potential to turn into something very rewarding.

Entrepreneurship is also one of the fastest ways to get rich. That's where the best of leveraging happens. Most of the investors trust human potential more than anything else, as it is other people that make their money for them.

Almost 90% of the billionaires have become rich by leveraging other people's money. Most billionaires' stories are usually rags to riches and there have been very few instances of heirs carrying a legacy forward.

Classically, Steve Jobs started out of a garage. So did Jeff Bezos. Mark Zuckerberg didn't have all the money to make it big; neither did Bill Gates nor did Warren Buffett. Almost all of them leveraged other people's money to become billionaires. It is not the most difficult thing to earn investors' trust, though it can sometimes become a long and arduous process.

But you should always have the edge, the extra something, the X factor to take that route.

However, this need not discourage you. Despite the need for market differentiation, you can also succeed if you are truly passionate about something. Even if your idea is not considered exciting by many, you will sure win, if you think your idea is worth billions and if you passionately work towards it.

Chapter 10

Buying Businesses (Owning Cash Flow Generating Assets)

Looking for well run businesses and buying partial or full stake in them can make you rich quite easily. You should just ensure that you get enough cash flow from the business. Owning, partially or fully, a well-run locally owned small business can be a good source of cash flow. It may also be easy to acquire adequate stake in a small business to get most of the profits flowing your way.

A local small business could be anything that could give you some cash flow. You may branch out as a franchiser and earn from more number of branches. A small business could range from gyms to coffee shops, dance schools, coaching classes, small IT/web designing firms, marketing agencies, PR firms, retail stores, car dealerships, car rentals, catering services, pin ball machines, fast food restaurants, etc.

Owning one to a few small businesses can be very rewarding. They may go on to make it big with franchisees all over the world.

They may also get listed in major stock markets all over the world. With small businesses, you can invest only very few thousand dollars. The size of your investment may grow into millions or even billions of dollars. This happens when people are willing to pay a higher price to buy your stock in order to own your business, if they believe that your business has the potential to grow multiple times its original size in the future.

Owning businesses is one of the best ways to improve your net worth. The investment can both appreciate as well as give you regular cash flow. Increasing your net worth via capital appreciation is the best thing that can happen to your investment. Most people do not realize that a high net worth is as important as cash flow. Many people associate getting rich only with cash flows.

Cash flow is very important. However, it is high net worth that makes you either a millionaire or a billionaire. Well, you actually need both and cash flow should come from the assets you own. Most people don't realize that owning a certain stake or equity in a business is also an asset.

If you want to quit the business, you may be able to sell your stake hundred to thousand to ten thousand times bigger than what you originally purchased it for.

Constantly looking out for such kind of opportunities coupled with a shift in your perspective and attitude towards money, business and other people will sure make you rich in the shortest possible time!

Chapter 11

Seeing Money Differently

In order to get rich, we should change our attitude towards money, business and other people in general. This change can open up both our brains and a lot of doorways for us to make money. If we have only a very narrow understanding or attitude towards money, we will neither make enough money nor get rich ever.

First, we should overcome the cause and effect relationship we believe of money that got so ingrained in us due to the Industrial Revolution and false socialistic belief patterns. Changing this attitude towards money will go a long way in making you rich in the shortest possible time. The act, the process or the event of getting rich happens not by way of what you do but what you choose to do and how you choose to do it. The paradigm shift in attitude from the linear and simplistic cause and effect (work and reward) assumptions on money to embracing the slight grey area around how money is made can make you rich.

Because business isn't a science but more of an art, there will always be some grey area around money.

Sales is not perfect logistics where all manufactured goods reach pre-assigned consumers by default. Only through a socialistic approach, by getting the government to make the purchase of some commodity or service mandatory, can you ever make sales a default process. This, though, is not always advisable.

No democratic population would like this being enforced on them. They will develop resentment and begin to revolt. So, sales should always involve some form of trickery and strategy, which we do not learn at school.

Schools would always teach you what can show definitive results like 2+2=4. Since they don't know if all sales effort will produce the same results, they won't teach you how to sell. Not all of us get to go to business schools, where this would usually be taught. With sales, you can't predict how, how much and how exactly your product will sell.

You can't be sure who will buy your product, especially when you are selling online. You neither know your customers nor see them.

This does not mean, though, that you have to see your customers in person or through any other means to sell. Make no mistake about it. Technologies like video conferencing, virtual reality, etc. may help you sell better. And since we are talking about getting rich and since most of getting rich happens through passive income, sales should happen, even if you don't employ your physical presence.

You may even work hard to understand consumer behavior, package your product well and work out a strategy to attract your customers but you can never say you will sell 175,317 units of a product. Despite the uncertainty, you can improve your confidence on yourself, your product and the market by providing a high quality product and marketing your products wisely.

So, as you begin to learn about money, you will get more of an abstract idea of money, which you will be able to make sense of. Then, the understanding will attain a definite solid form.

We need it to attain a solid form as almost all of us are used to right angled shapes and objects and not raw materials, which may be in the form of powder, wood, liquid, oil, glass, iron, etc.

We are also misled by appearances. Since we are consumers by default, we see only the finished product. We don't see what goes into making the product. Similarly, we do not also know what goes on in the background before and after the product is sold. How many of us learn or even think about what processes a particular product had to go through to finally find a place on the racks of a supermarket? The truth is majority of us don't. We do not also know what kind of sales psychology or tactics go into selling us the product. We do not know how the seller makes money. Even worse, we do not know nor learn how we have lost money!

That's why a shift in your perspective is very important because *getting rich happens not by way of what you do but what you choose to do and how you choose to do it!*

"Making It" Easy!

This book is designed to give you an easy perspective to help you with your understanding of money and your attitude towards it. I've explained — in the book — the very common limiting beliefs that I grew up with and how we can change the way we think to overcome them. Till I changed my perspectives and attitudes toward money, I was in a state of complete ignorance.

By the time I graduated and started "working in businesses", I could only treat business like work. That's all I knew about business. I didn't know I had to "work on my business."

Getting paid wasn't also that straightforward in business, as it appears to be in a job. That led me to explore why it wasn't working, what actually would work and how our limiting beliefs and attitudes prevented us from making money and getting rich!

I learned that people who were the most broke had the most of limiting beliefs and attitudes. Most of them could never even learn. So, I took it upon myself to break the patterns and set myself free. And I guess you can too! So, best of luck on your journey to the riches!

Works Cited
Bibliography

Anthony, Zane, Kathryn Sanders and David A. Fahrenthold. "Whatever happened to Trump neckties? They're over. So is most of Trump's merchandising empire." 13 April 2018. The Washington Post. 2 September 2018 <https://www.washingtonpost.com/politics/whatever-happened-to-trump-ties-theyre-over-so-is-most-of-trumps-merchandising-empire/2018/04/13/2c32378a-369c-11e8-acd5-35eac230e514_story.html?noredirect=on&utm_term=.955b5c14c1a8>.

Graham, Benjamin. The Intelligent Investor. Harper & Brothers, 1949.

Kiyosaki, Robert. Rich Dad Poor Dad: What The Rich Teach Their Kids About Money That The Poor And Middle Class Do Not! Scottsdale: Plata Publishing, LLC, 2011.

Nazari, Vazrick. "Review of Neopalpa Povolný, 1998 with description of a new species from California and Baja California, Mexico (Lepidoptera, Gelechiidae)." 17 January 2017. ZooKeys. 2 September 2018

<https://zookeys.pensoft.net/article/11411/list/1/>.

The Aviator. By John Logan. Dir. Martin Scorsese. Perf. Leonardo DiCaprio and John C. Reilly. Prods. Michael Mann, et al. Warner Bros. Pictures, 2004.

Thompson, Bill. "Fossil Echinoids of Texas A Monograph of Fossil Sea Urchins." 2016. ResearchGate. 2 September 2018 <https://www.researchgate.net/publication/310479936_Fossil_Echinoids_of_Texas_A_Monograph_of_Fossil_Sea_Urchins>.

Trump, Donald J. and Tony Schwartz. Trump: The Art of the Deal. Ballantine Books, 1987.

www.ingramcontent.com/pod-product-compliance
Lightning Source LLC
Chambersburg PA
CBHW030456220526
45464CB00006B/2558